DIDEROT'S *VIE DE SÉNÈQUE*

A Swan Song Revised

by Douglas A. Bonneville

Series: Florida. University, Gainesville
University of Florida Monographs,
Humanities

UNIVERSITY OF FLORIDA PRESS / GAINESVILLE, 1966

f 6/23/66

EDITORIAL COMMITTEE

Humanities Monographs

AS
36
.F58
No.19

AUTHOR'S NOTE

In the quotations from the French in this study there are numerous inconsistencies in spelling and punctuation. In every case I have endeavored to reproduce the text exactly, without regard to modern usage and without expletive notes. I should like to thank the readers of the typescript for finding many such inconsistencies and thus helping me to eliminate any that were not in the original texts. I accept full responsibility for any errors of transcription which remain.

I should like to express my appreciation to Professor Arthur Wilson and to Professor George Havens for their encouragement in the undertaking of this study. I hope that in a small way it reflects their own dedication to scholarship.

Thanks to Mr. Ray Jones, Research Librarian at the University of Florida, for locating and reproducing the original editions.

To Ann, for the patient deciphering and transcription of my *brouillons*, my deepest gratitude.

Thanks to the Graduate School of the University of Florida for making possible the publication of the monograph.

D.A.B.

CONTENTS

1. THE PROBLEM
OF THE TEXTS

Although the *Essai sur les règnes de Claude et de Néron* was the last of Diderot's long works and was important enough, in his opinion, to warrant a major revision less than four years after its first publication, there is no comparative study of the two texts.[1] All critical treatments of the work, except for the polemics resulting from its initial appearance, have been based on the second edition alone. La Harpe's effort to refute, point by point, the apology for Seneca's life, is perhaps the best complete summary of all objections raised against the *Essai*, and is, in fact, a lengthy but accurate statement of its general critical reputation, which has never been high.[2] Fritz Schalk's excellent monograph is the first attempt since the eighteenth century to study the work on its own merits.[3] Herr Schalk, though confining himself to the second edition, considers its reception, history, structure, style, major themes, and general

1. The first edition, published in December, 1778, bears the date 1779 and is entitled *Essai sur la vie de Sénèque le philosophe, sur ses écrits, et sur les règnes de Claude et de Néron*. Though it is the seventh volume of La Grange's translation of Seneca's works, the *Essai* was also available separately, according to the "Catalogue" appended to it by the publisher, De Bure. This original version was reprinted at least once, in 1789. The second edition appeared in 1782, claiming to have been printed in London. Entitled *Essai sur les règnes de Claude et de Néron, et sur les mœurs et les écrits de Sénèque*, it is the only generally available text, since it has been consistently reproduced by Naigeon and his successors. It originally comprised two volumes.

2. Jean-François de la Harpe, *Lycée, ou cours de littérature ancienne et moderne*, Paris, Agasse, an VII—an XIII [1799-1805], III, 160-347. See also XVI, 295-313, of the same work, and his *Correspondance littéraire adressée à son Altesse Impériale* . . . Paris, Migneret, 1804-7, II, 234 ff., 327; III, 347-49. The long discussion in volume III of the *Lycée* is in the section entitled "Anciens" and purports to be a study of Seneca, but is actually a broadside attack on Diderot. Though obviously prejudiced, the treatment is an interesting and readable statement of the more current eighteenth-century view of Seneca.

3. *Diderots Essai über Claudius und Nero*, Köln, Westdeutscher Verlag, 1956.

1

significance, laying special stress on its richness in the time concepts so brilliantly set forth by Georges Poulet.[4] J. Robert Loy, finally, suggests that the *Essai* may be the long moral treatise that Diderot had envisioned during his whole life.[5] Except for these critical studies, references to the work are incidental and limited to fragments: the note on Rousseau, the comments on Voltaire, the statements about time, politics, and immortality.

The question of the two editions is not complicated. The second version, essentially an elaboration of the first edition of 1778, has been constantly republished in the same form since its appearance in 1782.[6] Naigeon, who edited the work in both its first publications, also gave it its definitive shape when he brought out his edition of Diderot's complete works.[7] Brière annotated the *Essai* and listed the sources of some of the polemics.[8] Assézat incorporated all of Brière's notes into his edition, added his own comments, and pointed out a few, but very few, of the changes Diderot had made in the work.[9] This last-named text is the most readily available and the most completely explicated, but in addition to the fact that its comparison of the two versions is haphazard, it fails to show any of the minor changes that Naigeon, in typical fashion, seems to have made on his own.

Naigeon's alterations are not unjustifiable. He was, after all, the editor of the first editions, and had dedicated to him the preface to the 1778 text and those to both parts of the revision.[10] Indeed, Diderot literally surrenders the text to

4. *Etudes sur le temps humain*, Paris, Plon, 1950.
5. "L'Essai sur les règnes de Claude et de Néron," *Cahiers de l'Association Internationale des Etudes Françaises*, juin, 1961 (XIII), 239-54. A discussion of the papers presented is on pp. 396-99 of the same issue. 6. See note 1.
7. *Œuvres de Denis Diderot*, publiées sur les manuscrits de l'auteur, par Jacques-André Naigeon . . . Paris, Déterville, an VII [1798], VIII and IX.
8. *Œuvres de Denis Diderot*, Paris, J. L. J. Brière, 1821-23, XI and XII.
9. *Œuvres Complètes de Diderot*, revues sur les éditions originales . . . par J. Assézat et M. Tourneux, Paris, Garnier, 1875-77, III. Hereafter, A-T, III.
10. For some reason Assézat indicates in a note that the dedication of the

Naigeon when he says to the editor, "disposez de mon travail comme il vous plaira; vous êtes le maître d'approuver, de contredire, d'ajouter, de retrancher" (11; I, 5; 7).[11] Naigeon takes him at his word, adding note after lengthy note to both editions, carefully distinguishing his own comments from Diderot's. He is, however, less careful when he edits Diderot's complete works. In two cases, for example, Naigeon seems deliberately to have deleted two comments favorable to the critic La Harpe, no doubt in revenge for the treatment Diderot had received in the *Lycée.* Speaking of Rousseau's vaunted eloquence, Diderot claims in 1782 to prefer *"l'Eloge de Fénelon,* celui *de Marc Aurèle,* et quelques pages à choix de *l'Histoire naturelle* à tous les ouvrages de Rousseau" (95; I, 132). The *Eloge de Fénelon,* by La Harpe, is no doubt the same one Diderot had maltreated in the *Correspondance littéraire.*[12] Before assuming that Diderot made a mistake, it must be considered that he had never denied the eloquence of La Harpe's work, only its feeling.

---

first part did not appear in the 1778 edition (A-T, III, 9). Actually, it did, though it read "A M. N° ° °." The preface to the second part was also in the original, but integrated into the text as a transitional paragraph, and not as a separate notice. Why it should have been dedicated separately to Naigeon in the revision is not clear.

11. Here and henceforth the first number in parentheses will refer to the page in A-T, III, the second to the volume and page in the 1782 edition, and the third, when it occurs, to the page in the 1778 edition.

12. *Correspondance littéraire* . . . par Grimm, Diderot, *et al.,* revue sur les textes originaux . . . par Maurice Tourneux, Paris, Garnier, 1877-82, IX, 383. Diderot's observations on La Harpe's *Eloge* had appeared eleven years before, in November, 1771. Of interest here, too, is the following epigram which La Harpe turned at Naigeon's expense; and which could hardly have improved relations between the two men.

> Je suis philosophe et je m'en pique,
> Et tout le monde le sait;
> Je vis de métaphysique,
> De légumes et de lait.
> J'ai reçu de la nature
> Une figure à bonbon;
> Ajoutez-y ma frisure
> Et je suis monsieur Naigeon.

(*Correspondance littéraire,* XIII, 187.)

Whatever the reasons for the qualified praise, Naigeon withdraws it by substituting in his edition the *Eloge de Descartes*, by Thomas, who had also written that of Marcus Aurelius. Later, in a note, Diderot refers to La Harpe's theft and publication of Voltaire's *Guerre de Genève* as a "légère inadvertence" for which the unfortunate La Harpe had been treated too cruelly (179; I, 342).[13] Naigeon obviously is of another opinion when he omits the allusion in his edition. Of the two quotations which follow, the first is from the edition of 1782 and the second from Naigeon's collection.

> En voici un autre qui reparaît, tenant en main une satyre de Voltaire, de M. de la Harpe, qui saura bien le châtier, s'il le croit digne de sa férule, des *Muses Rivales*, et d'un public imbécile qui s'obstine à applaudir un poëme charmant, et composé long-temps avant la légère inadvertence qu'on lui a si cruellement reprochée, avec un parallele de Plutarque et de Sénèque, écrit par le poëte Dryden (I, 342).

> Après avoir fait ci-dessus la critique aussi sévère que juste d'une note que j'ai écrite il y a plus de trente-six ans; après avoir, par un désaveu public et sincère, expié en quelque sorte cette faute de ma jeunesse, je vais examiner avec la même impartialité un parallèle de Plutarque et de Sénèque écrit par le poëte Dryden, et que quelques censeurs aussi inconsidérés, aussi peu instruits que je l'étais alors, ont cité contre Sénèque (179).

Since Diderot died in 1784, it is doubtful that he would have had either the occasion or any reason for changing the note. It is therefore probable that Naigeon made the changes

13. For Grimm's version of the theft of the manuscript, see the *Correspondance littéraire*, VIII, 49-50. I have been unable to find the "satyre" mentioned in the following quotation or to identify the "autre" [monstre?] who presumably was its author. The *Muses rivales*, by La Harpe, is a one-act play in verse in which the muses dispute as to which one may claim Voltaire.

himself in the guise of Diderot. Without laboring this particular point, it seems apparent that if a comparison is to be made of the two versions, it should be based on the originals.

Reasons for the lack of general public interest in the work are easy to summarize: on the one hand the subject seems distant and academic, and on the other the style is apparently digressive, the tone quarrelsome and even peevish.[14] In short, the *Essai* is bland literary fare at best for the admirer of *Jacques le fataliste* and has little of the philosophical rigor and brilliance which attracts the reader to the *Lettre sur les aveugles or the Rêve de d'Alembert*. Scholarly unconcern for the work, however, is more difficult to explain. To be sure, the second edition seems merely to stretch the original, almost always by adding to it and only rarely changing it; but the additions virtually double its length. Such a body of material would merit examination by virtue of its bulk alone. Besides the quantitative reason, though, there is more substantial motivation for comparing the two texts. Because the work came late in Diderot's life, because it underwent extensive revision, because it is basically ethical and personal in inspiration, it has obvious biographical implications. Just the fact that it is widely quoted is a recommendation for study. Is Georges Poulet, who cites numerous passages from the *Essai* in his *Etudes sur le temps humain*, quoting the Diderot of 1778 or 1782? If time is really of the essence, the distinction might well be valid, not only in Poulet's study, but in those of Henri Lefebvre, I. K. Luppol, and the many others who have had recourse to the work. Also of importance is the fact that the much publicized comment on Rousseau, which grew from a page-long footnote to several pages of text, has never been closely studied for the

14. See Schalk, 5-10, however, for an account of the lively interest aroused by the *Essai* on its first publication. Roland Mortier treats the spirited German polemic inspired by the work in his *Diderot en Allemagne* (1750-1850), Paris, Presses Universitaires de France, 1954, 197-209.

significance of the changes in it. Then, too, both M. Jean Fabre and Mr. Loy have agreed to the need for a comparison of the two editions, and their opinion bears consideration.[15] Finally, like the mountain, the unexplored text is *there* and challenges by its very presence.

Before proceeding further, I should like to point out that there is in my opinion no fundamental change of either structure or content in the second edition. There are still two main parts: Seneca's life and times are the subject of the first, and his writings, of the second. The general arrangement by topics is retained, as is the *Promenade* structure suggested by Herr Schalk.[16] In both editions Seneca is more or less Diderot, Rome is more or less Paris, and divergences in both cases are made clear. Nor is the constant shift from one level of time to the other of greater or less importance in the revision. As to personalities, Suilius and Rousseau are consistently villains, Seneca and Diderot always heroes. Again and again the author treats the same themes: politics, philosophy, morality, style, personal relations, and reputation. Stylistically, digression, flashback, use of dialogue, intrusion, apostrophe, irony, antithesis, and so forth are proportionately no greater in either edition; and the fact should surprise no one, for these devices had long since been brought to perfection in the writings of Diderot.

There are, however, three obvious differences between the editions of 1778 and 1782: a change of title, a doubling of length, and a sharpening of tone. I shall discuss these variants in the order I have mentioned them and try to establish whatever relation they bear to one another. Inasmuch as both originals are rare, and the first is, so to speak, included in the second, page references are to the standard Assézat edition, then to the earlier ones, with variants pointed out in footnotes.

15. See the discussion in *CAIEF*, juin, 1961 (XIII), 396-97.   16. Schalk, 14.

2. THE CHANGE OF TITLE

The change of title at first glance appears to provide rich ground for speculation: the emphasis of the earlier title, *Essai sur la vie de Sénèque le philosophe, sur ses écrits, et sur les règnes de Claude et de Néron*,[1] is obviously on Seneca the man, whereas the second, *Essai sur les règnes de Claude et de Néron, et sur les mœurs et les écrits de Sénèque, pour servir d'introduction à la lecture de ce philosophe*,[2] implies a subordination of the individual to socio-political factors. Now, Diderot is not one for resounding titles, as his *Satire seconde* and *Sur l'inconséquence du jugement public de nos actions particulières* well illustrate. Moreover, in the final pages of the later edition he refers to his work as the *Essai sur les mœurs de Sénèque*, indicating that he might have been uncertain himself as to what to entitle it. If the difference is less important than it may at first seem, however, the cardinal fact remains: the title was changed, during Diderot's lifetime, and apparently with his approval.[3] It may also be pointed out that the emphasis shifts from the philosopher Seneca to his times, and that the word *mœurs* is added, introducing a moral note. That Diderot was not entirely unaware of the significance of the change of title is demonstrated by a note added to the second edition in justification of a long digression on the character and actions of Claudius: "Si l'on se rappelle le titre de cet Essai, et si l'on ne confond pas le fond avec l'accessoire, on ne sera pas surpris de cet écart" (38; I, 293).[4]

1. See note 1 to Chapter 1.
2. See note 1 to Chapter 1 and note 2 to Chapter 4.
3. Unlike the titles of the *Neveu de Rameau* and *Mme de la Carlière*, which he had no chance to consider.
4. In the edition of 1782, this note is specifically attributed to Diderot, but in Naigeon's *Œuvres*, the editor claims it.

3. THE LONG
INTERPOLATIONS

As to the difference in length of the two editions, it is accounted for by six long additions to the text and innumerable shorter ones, consisting of from one or two sentences to several paragraphs. Of the three long interpolations mentioned by Assézat, the first is devoted to the introduction into the text of the famous note on Rousseau, with justificatory comment by Diderot, the second to an imaginary reprimand administered by the author to one of his critics, and the last to a defense of Diderot as the author of the original *Essai sur la vie de Sénèque*.

Since the note on Rousseau and its justification have received their due,[1] I shall discuss only the significance of the

1. Although the 1782 remarks on Rousseau in themselves seem to offer little more than proof of Diderot's growing self-concern, they have inspired considerable controversy since their appearance. It is worth noting that even the second edition of the *Essai* almost certainly appeared before the publication of the first six volumes of Rousseau's *Confessions* and that Diderot could not therefore have read them before revising his note of 1778. The *Essai sur les règnes de Claude et de Néron* is reviewed in the *Correspondance littéraire* in March, 1782 (XIII, 103-5), and was thus published early in that year. The first half of the *Confessions* is reviewed by the *Correspondance littéraire* in July of the same year (XIII, 160-67), and in the *Correspondance secrète* of Métra, May 22, 1782 (Londres, 1788, XIII, 46-49). Most critics now accept the opinion of Théophile Dufour: "La première partie des *Confessions* (Livre I-VI) a paru probablement en avril 1782, en tout cas avant le 18 mai" (*Recherches bibliographiques sur les œuvres imprimées de J.-J. Rousseau*, Paris, 1925, I, 238). See as well the discussion of the topic in volume I of the Pléiade edition of Rousseau's *Œuvres complètes*, Paris, Gallimard, 1959, 1889-91.

A second note on Rousseau, sometimes attributed to Diderot, is found at the end of the first part of both editions. It is consistently claimed by the editor, and as Assézat remarks, there is no reason for confusion on this point (196-98; I, 352-56; 241-45).

See Mortier, 197-209, for a typical, if selective, treatment of the note. For the history of the relationship consult Norman L. Torrey, "Rousseau's Quarrel with Diderot and Grimm," *Yale Romanic Studies*, 1943 (XXII), 163-82. The

part added in 1782. The addition is as interesting for what it reveals about Diderot as for what it says about Jean-Jacques. Grimm considers the 1782 discussion to be a softening of a rather severe criticism: "L'apologie de Sénèque est devenue plus complète, ou du moins plus ingénieuse, la diatribe contre J.-J. Rousseau, diatribe qu'on avait trouvée si révoltante, beaucoup plus étendue, mieux motivée et par là même peut-être moins violente, moins odieuse."[2] Mr. Loy is of the opposite conviction: "Toutefois faut-il tenir compte de la différence entre le passage sur Rousseau de la première édition de l'*Essai* et ceux de la deuxième édition, beaucoup plus cruels, mal avisés et pleins d'une émotion peu conforme au goût de l'écrivain sérieux et qui entend nous entretenir de vérités universelles."[3] The significance of the revision, I feel, is not in the attitude toward Rousseau, which does not change noticeably, but in the style of Diderot, which does.

The original note is a direct, deliberately ill-concealed allusion to the Genevan. Diderot's denial that such a monster could exist is, of course, rhetorical, and serves only to emphasize Rousseau's baseness. The whole passage is one long, unrelieved paragraph of abuse. As for the commentary of 1782, it consists of a sanctimonious hand-washing ceremony and further, by now quite direct, vilification. If the shoe fits, wear it, he advises Jean-Jacques' "fanatics," as he exonerates himself from any self-interest: "Non, censeurs, non; ce n'est point la crainte d'être maltraité dans l'écrit posthume de Jean-Jacques qui m'a fait parler. Je vous suis mal connu. Je savais par un des hommes les plus véridiques, M. Dusaulx, de l'Académie des inscriptions, et par d'autres personnes à qui Rousseau n'avait pas dédaigné de lire ses *Confessions*,

---

latter work does not mention the *Essai*. See also Lord Morley's *Diderot and the Encyclopedists* in his *Works*, London, Macmillan, 1921 (XI, 179), and Lester Crocker's *The Embattled Philosopher; a Life of Denis Diderot*, East Lansing, Michigan State College Press, 1954, 424-25.

2. *Correspondance littéraire*, XIII, 103-4.   3. Loy, 244.

que j'étais malheureusement épargné entre un grand nombre de personnes qu'il y déchirait. Cette fois je n'étais que le vengeur d'autrui" (93; I, 129-30). But despite these protestations of selflessness he concludes the commentary with a remark which seems much more to the point: "Ce n'est point une satire que j'écris, c'est mon apologie, c'est celle d'un assez grand nombre de citoyens qui me sont chers" (99; I, 139). And in fact Diderot seems more interested in absolving himself of guilt than in anything else. If he paints Rousseau blacker, it is so that he, Diderot, will appear whiter; the greater Jean-Jacques' villainy, the more noble is Diderot's defense of outraged innocence. This opinion is not gratuitous; it is made plausible by this addition, in 1782, to the preface of the first part: "l'on ne tardera pas à s'apercevoir que c'est autant mon âme que je peins, que celle des différents personnages qui s'offrent à mon récit" (10; I, 4), and is borne out, as will be shown below, in most of what was added to the original edition.

Second in importance to the justification of his note on Rousseau is his long defense of the original *Essai*. Appended to the second part, this addition, as Brière and Assézat after him demonstrate, is a selective listing of objections which appeared in current journals, Marmontel's answers to the objections, and Diderot's further comments, most of which are introduced by "j'ajouterai." The tone of the entire section is one of martyrdom, as is reflected in Diderot's decision to have Marmontel's comments justify him rather than merely his own. Those critics who wish to prove Diderot's disillusionment with his contemporary public or his conviction that he sacrificed his literary talents to encyclopedic hack work have rich ground for substantiating quotations. When Marmontel points to the twenty-five years "consacrées à ébaucher l'histoire de la philosophie, et la description des arts mécaniques," which served to enrich only the

10

booksellers and not Diderot, a sacrifice of time and self appreciated only by Catherine, Diderot, tearfully and modestly, adds: "Et *j'ajouterai* que je sais, à la vérité, un assez grand nombre de choses, mais il n'y a presque pas un homme qui ne sache sa chose beaucoup mieux que moi. Cette médiocrité dans tous les genres est la suite d'une curiosité effrénée et d'une fortune si modique qu'il ne m'a jamais été permis de me livrer tout entier à une seule branche de la connaissance humaine" (400-401; II, 314). In a welter of self-effacement he then takes credit only for being a "passable moraliste," and hopes that in condemning him for whatever he lacks as an apologist for Seneca, his readers will condemn neither his cause nor the truly great men with whom he is associated through his apology.[4]

According to Diderot, he has let Marmontel take his defense "un peu par vanité," but mostly to set off against one another the different opinions of his work, to show "combien il importe de ne pas s'en rapporter à d'autres, si l'on veut avoir son opinion" (380-81; II, 285). Then, as if in spite of himself, he provides a guide for the reader in the form of a questionnaire containing three questions about Seneca and seven about Diderot. And in fact the percentage thus represented might, conservatively, be said to reflect the relative emphasis placed on author and subject in the long additions of the 1782 edition. The final three paragraphs reiterate the plea for impartial and independent judgment, but the last sentence, "Si le dernier qui parle est celui qui a raison, censeurs, parlez, et ayez raison" (407; II, 324), is one of disgruntlement, weariness, and pessimism, and reaffirms the personal note of peevishness apparent throughout the long passage.[5] From this it seems clear that the emphasis

4. He names Tacitus, Tertullian, Bishop Otto of Freising, Montaigne, and La Mothe Le Vayer.
5. The sentence might nicely be contrasted with Rameau's parting jibe, "Rira bien qui rira le dernier."

of these two long additions is on neither Seneca nor his times, but rather on Diderot and his. Rousseau is condemned, Voltaire and d'Holbach are defended;[6] Tacitus, Claudius, and Nero are virtually ignored.

The other long addition indicated in Assézat displays a basically contemporary interest (65-79; I, 83-109). It is in fact made up of several successive interpolations of varying length, but separated by only short paragraphs of the original text. Sections of the first part of this addition, as Assézat points out, appeared in the *Correspondance littéraire* as a response to criticism by l'abbé Grosier, and largely form an apology for Seneca's conduct.[7] The accusations and exonerations do not vary considerably from those mentioned in the other interpolations. Charged with hypocrisy, opportunism, and condoning of evil, Seneca is justified on the grounds that he had been responsible for the five good years of Nero's reign and would better serve Rome by remaining in public life and trying to effect reform than by retiring or dying a suicide or martyr.

The second part is more general and compares Rome and France in the area of royal favorites. "Dans un Etat purement monarchique, tel que la France, une maîtresse avare ou dissipatrice ruine le peuple" (71; I, 95).

A third part opens with a justification of Seneca's friendship with Serenus, a court libertine. Diderot denies that there is any guilt by mere association, then adds that one couldn't have lived in Nero's profligate court without forming some questionable relationships, even intimate ones. Typically, he uses this criterion of relativism to launch into a discussion of the duel, of religious celibacy, and of customs in general, all of which must, according to Diderot, be considered in their social context.

6. A-T, III, 394-96, 385-87 for Voltaire and d'Holbach respectively; 1782, II, 303-8, 293-94.   7. XII, 297-302.

Both Seneca and Burrus are in this light absolved from guilt in the machinations of Agrippina and in her death. Diderot's reasoning seems to work this way: Agrippina was a schemer; Nero was incestuously attracted to her; abetted by Seneca and Burrus, she used this attraction to lure Nero away from a prostitute; to avoid the dilemma of incestuous love and the desire to escape parental domination, Nero killed Agrippina, without the intervention of either Seneca or Burrus. Incest, debauchery, and murderous intent all existed independently of the two ministers. No matter what they did, murder or incest would have resulted. The choice between murder and incest being absurd, Seneca and Burrus, in failing to choose, were guilty of nothing.

In this interpolation, then, the major considerations are personal and social morality, highlighted by a digression on royal favorites. What is most striking about the overall effect is its starkness. Seneca has a choice between living amidst corruption or abdicating his human responsibilities. The institution of royal favorites, rather than being condemned, is accepted as inevitable and then described in its effects on governments. The duels and other fundamentally odious social practices are simply inherent in the societies in which they exist. And the dilemma of incest and murder is presented in all its nakedness.

A fourth lengthy interpolation, not noted by Assézat, is found near the end of Part I and is devoted almost exclusively to Seneca, half to refuting his critics and half to quoting, paraphrasing, and elucidating his apologists. With characteristic aplomb Diderot takes on first that most formidable of all opponents, himself at the age of thirty.[8] To the young man's charge that Seneca was greedy for wealth,

8. As Assézat points out, Diderot's harsh youthful criticism of Seneca is to be found in the *Essai sur le mérite et la vertu* (A-T, I, 118). Diderot gives his age as thirty. In 1745, at the time of the publication of his reworking of Shaftesbury, he was actually thirty-two.

the sexagenarian replies, "Sénèque eut des richesses, mais il n'en eut pas la passion" (176; I, 252). An imputation that Seneca condoned by his silence the execution of innocent political victims is scornfully attributed to a false reading of history, which may in turn be blamed on a poor education.[9] When Seneca's offer to give his fortune to Nero is interpreted as an attempt to buy his life, it is made clear that the offer preceded the fear of being poisoned. A reference to Tacitus for proof is called a misreading of the historian (again blamed on his teachers), and a reflection on Seneca's honor is laid to youthful presumption and a failure to consider that all that was good about Nero's reign is directly attributable to his tutor. This "étourdi, en qui malheureusement quelque facilité d'écrire avait devancé le sens commun" (178; I, 256), the thirty-year-old Diderot, is thus condemned for inability to read Latin, careless scholarship, immaturity, and presumptuousness. Add "mauvaise foi" and you have a complete idea of what Diderot thinks of most of the detractors of Seneca.[10]

After next paying tribute to d'Holbach as an exception to the general run of Seneca's enemies, Diderot resumes his case. He confesses unashamedly that Seneca did indeed commit human errors, because he was human. Any moral inconsistencies, though, he attributes to ethical ambiguity, which he represents as the dilemma of the judge trying to decide between justice and mercy. Attacks on the stylistic frivolity of Seneca's philosophical writings are parried by the suggestion that the attackers lack literary sensitivity—

9. Diderot often criticizes his early education. Cf. Marmontel's remark, "Il sait le latin, bien qu'il ait passé dans les écoles de la Compagnie de Jésus, ainsi que beaucoup d'autres, sans en excepter les censeurs, cinq ou six années à l'étudier, sans l'avoir appris" (385; II, 292).

10. La Harpe argues that Diderot, having once taken a strong stand against Seneca, might well be less positive of the "mauvaise foi" of his critics. Actually, Diderot's technique neatly explains his own apparent self-contradiction and implies that those who hold the opinion that he once held are immature and ill-educated at best; otherwise they are liars.

14

and background. To the charge that Seneca, in outlining the calumnies to which he would be subjected as Nero's minister, is confessing his guilt, Diderot responds with a call to common sense. Complaints against Seneca's ministry are answered by allusion to the five "good years" with which it began. Seneca's phrase "le clément Néron" is explained as a current epithet. Generally speaking, then, all attacks against Seneca are made on a black-and-white basis and are answered by Diderot with a call for a relativistic perspective. His defense is based on arguments of moral ambiguity and political necessity, and he asks that accusations be dismissed for insufficient evidence and misreading of the facts.

On the affirmative side Diderot quotes Pliny to testify to Seneca's unworldliness, Tertullian to his piety, Bishop Otto of Freising and Erasmus to his "Christianity," Montaigne, his integrity, Plutarch, his philosophy, and Quintilian, his eloquence. Then, after a plea that Seneca's works, for both their moral and stylistic values, be included in the curriculum of the educational system, Diderot likens the critics of Seneca to Dion Cassius, and his apologists to Tacitus (176-82; I, 251-74).

The significance of this lengthy discussion is obviously neither in the force of Diderot's arguments nor in the validity of the character references he offers. Rather it would seem to be in the importance he attaches to the charges against Seneca. These charges—that Seneca was motivated by a desire for wealth, that he was a hypocrite, and that he was a coward—are considered over and over again. The constant repetition of the same accusations and the fact that Diderot has, since his youth, done a complete and irrevocable about-face on each one of them, force the question: why should they concern him? Some possible answers to the question will emerge from further comparison of the two editions of this *Essai*. One point seems to become increasingly clear: Diderot's role in this apology, at least in the second version, is equally as important as Seneca's. He is obviously worried about the publication of Rousseau's *Confessions;* he appears to be excessively disturbed by the personal attacks of Geoffroy, l'abbé Grosier, and others; and he is concerned enough about a forty-year-old slur he himself made on Seneca, and in a footnote at that, to recant publicly.

Another area of sensitivity, apparent in a fifth long addition (223-37; II, 40-64), is that of literary style. Diderot first denies a charge that Seneca lacks feeling in his *Consolation to Helvia,* citing Justus Lipsius' opinion that Seneca turns his mother's thoughts from the source of her grief to her only possible consolation, dedication to the rest of her family. Then he shows how Seneca consoled himself for his exile to Corsica: "Il observait la nature, il écrivait ses questions de physique, il composait des poëmes, il était occupé des peines de sa mère . . ." (226; II, 45). True consolation, by word and example, would thus be proof enough of Seneca's real sensitivity.

Seneca is further accused of unevenness of style, tediousness, fustian, excessive subtlety, lack of taste, and pretentiousness. But Diderot contends that unevenness is necessary to set off the essential. What might appear to be tediousness, he argues, is rather the deliberate discrimination between nuances of meaning. The charge of fustian is countered with an opinion to the contrary by Marmontel, who also happens to applaud Diderot's courageous role as apologist. As to the subtleties that are said to weaken the expression of Seneca's ideas, Diderot compares them to "l'humble violette qui, dans la forêt, croît au pied des grands arbres" (230; II, 51). They may distract the eye momentarily, but they have an undeniable beauty of their own. Seneca's alleged lack of taste is then likened to Voltaire's, and both allegations are sum-

16

marily dismissed. Finally, in response to the accusation that Seneca is pretentious, Diderot declares: "Sénèque parle d'après la chaleur de son âme et l'élévation de son caractère. S'il étincelle, c'est comme le diamant ou les astres, dont la nature est d'étinceler. Le reprendre d'une affectation de briller, c'est reprocher à l'hirondelle la légèreté de son vol: il a le ton du bel esprit comme un autre a le ton de la suffisance, sans s'en douter" (232; II, 54). It is noteworthy that in these remarks on style Diderot, uncharacteristically, has recourse to images, and that the three cited above are taken from nature.[11] If not striking or original, they are apt.

Stylistically, Fritz Schalk has compared the writings of Diderot and Seneca.[12] It takes no inquisitive mind to ask whether the charges leveled against the Roman might also have been aimed at the Frenchman, whether, in fact, Diderot was defending his own writings. At any rate, he decides that Seneca "serait bien plus fâché d'avoir fait un mauvais raisonnement qu'une mauvaise phrase" (232; II, 56). And once again he gives a series of pro-Senecan quotations from other authorities, digressing briefly to praise Montaigne for a passage containing the very "faults" from which Seneca had just been absolved.

A final interpolation, arising from Seneca's *Natural Questions*, demonstrates Diderot's scientific preoccupations (358-66; II, 253-67). He prefaces his comments, however, with a brief attempt to explain away Seneca's dedicatory remark to Nero. "Vous avez . . . un goût pour la vérité aussi vif que pour les autres vertus . . ." (358; II, 253). The explanation, if it may be called such, is a series of rather lame questions and irrelevant hypotheses: "Mais de quelles vertus s'agit-il ici? Quelle est la date de cet écrit? Est-ce un éloge? est-ce une leçon? On peut haïr un homme vertueux dont la

11. Eric Steele, *Diderot's Imagery: A Study of Literary Personality*, New York, Corporate Press, 1941, 126-65.   12. Schalk, 22-23.

présence nous en impose; mais je ne crois pas que le plus méchant des hommes puisse haïr la vertu et la vérité, non plus que trouver beau ce qui est hideux" (358; II, 253-54). More interesting, though no more relevant, is the query: "L'histoire, l'expérience ne nous apprennent-elles point à distinguer différentes époques dans la vie des rois?" (358; II, 254). The obvious implication of the question will be made clearer in a discussion of Diderot's socio-political concerns in 1782.

What interests the apologist most in the *Natural Questions* is the tempering of science with morality. The scientific inadequacy of the work is blamed on the premature rise of "rational physics," which logically should have appeared only after experimental physics had prepared the way. In a long paragraph, one of the few optimistic additions of the 1782 edition, Diderot sketches the progress of experimental physics toward the discovery of the unknown.

Turning rather abruptly from physics, he then considers some of Seneca's thoughts on omens and destiny. To the Roman's objective observation that the cry of a crow or an owl is not a sign of misfortune, Diderot more objectively adds that man's apparent preoccupation with unhappy signs is in curious contradiction with his usually heedless quest for small pleasures. When Seneca suggests, however, that lightning is the most powerful of presages, Diderot, instead of denying omens as might be expected, declares such signs to be as valid as belief in gods. "Un système de mensonges ressemble plus à la vérité qu'un seul mensonge isolé," he declares, defending omens less than attacking religious dogma (361; II, 259). And having broached the subject of religion, he quotes, virtually without commentary, a number of anti-religious, stoic thoughts.

The addition terminates with two apparently unconnected anecdotes, one in praise of Muret, a sixteenth-century humanist who, according to Diderot, saved the life of an "âme vile" on whom doctors were going to perform a perilous experiment, and the other in condemnation of Seneca for insidiously flattering Lucilius, telling him not to hesitate to praise himself, advising him to distrust flatterers, and complimenting him on his modesty.[13]

Of all the interpolations considered so far, this one seems to hang together least well. There are at least five separate parts: the justification of Seneca's praise of Nero, the tribute to Seneca's dual role of scientist and moralist, the dissertation on rational and experimental physics, the remarks on popular superstitions, and the anecdotes. Any unifying element would have to be thematic. One possible theme implicit in all five divisions is the cleavage between appearance and reality. Prefaces are, after all, often pretexts, and irony can be either intended or unconscious; the apparent logic of rational physics is continually broken down by experiment; omens and rites may or may not be valid, depending on whether they coincide with destiny; Diderot might have been aware of the possibility that the "âme vile" whom Muret saved was Muret himself; and Seneca's flattery was avowedly "très-délié" because it paraded as sincerity. The idea is at least intriguing and not at all uncharacteristic of Diderot.

13. For further explanation of the Muret anecdote, see A-T, III, 362-63, *notes*.

4. THE CHANGES
IN POLITICAL ATTITUDE

So much for the six long interpolated passages. Taken as a whole they may be said to summarize the themes and give the tone of the changes made to the first edition. But they still comprise only 150 out of the total of 300 pages by which the first edition was increased. The rest of the interpolations, varying from a sentence or two to several paragraphs in length, thus account for half of the bulk. I have grouped them into loose categories, many of which overlap, but which have been chosen to show the relative emphasis of each addition. These categories are: socio-political, moral, philosophical, stylistic, and personal. Some of them may be divided into sub-categories.

The socio-political category, for example, can be broken down into those passages which compare ancient Rome and eighteenth-century France, and those which express general views on such topics as monarchy, social institutions, and the class struggle. The parallel between Rome under Claudius and Nero and France under the aging Louis XIV and Louis XV is obvious and has been mentioned elsewhere.[1] But the manner in which Diderot modifies his commentary in the second edition is not made clear. There is, for one thing, between the treatments of politics in the two editions, a marked increase in bitterness. Writing of Seneca's father in 1778, for example, Diderot states, "Il avait recueilli les harangues grecques et latines de plus de cent orateurs fameux sous le règne d'Auguste. . . ." But in 1782 he adds, "Cent orateurs fameux sous le seul règne d'Auguste! Quelle épi-

1. By Grimm, La Harpe, Schalk, Loy, and others.

démie! Depuis la renaissance des lettres jusqu'à nos jours, l'Europe entière n'en fournirait pas autant" (16; I, 11). Explicitly the moderns suffer by comparison; implicitly, so does eighteenth-century France. Later, describing the many wise and just moves made by Claudius on his accession to the throne of empire, Diderot remarks, "Les meilleures opérations se font quelquefois sous les plus mauvais règnes, et réciproquement" (34; I, 37). Again by implication, eighteenth-century France is condemned in either case. More directly, Diderot writes in 1778, "Claude n'est rien sur le trône." (Note the use of the present tense: Louis XVI was crowned in 1774.)[2] And in 1782, after adding a list of examples of Claudius' timidity, he concludes, "La faiblesse qui ne sait ni empêcher le mal, ni ordonner le bien, multiplie la tyrannie" (37; I, 41).[3] If the use of the present tense is a subtle allusion to Louis XVI, or XV, the maxim is an outright condemnation of the kind of leadership with which France was afflicted throughout the Age of Ideas.

Seemingly getting bolder as he continues to revise, Dide-

---

2. Cf. *Correspondance littéraire* (XIII, 104-5), which explicitly states the political overtones: "Cette nouvelle édition de l'*Essai sur Sénèque* n'ayant paru que sous une permission tacite, l'auteur a eu la liberté d'y insérer beaucoup de choses qu'il avait été forcé de supprimer dans la première; on pourra même trouver que cette liberté a été portée fort loin dans plusieurs endroits, comme dans le parallèle du caractère de Claude et de celui d'un roi qu'il n'est pas difficile de reconnaître, puisqu'on lui cite des mots connus de tout le monde.

"Claude, dit l'apologiste de Sénèque, Claude n'est rien sur le trône, rien dans le palais, il le sait, il l'avoue. Il eût dit de deux édifices publics dont on lui aurait présenté des modèles: *Voilà le plus beau, mais ce n'est pas celui qu'ils choisiront.* Il eût dit d'un de ses ministres: *Il faudra bien qu'il succombe, il n'y a que moi qui le soutiens.* Faible mais sensé, s'il eût opiné dans son conseil il eût dit: *Mon avis est le meilleur, ils ne l'ont pas suivi, je crois qu'ils s'en repentiront.* Il disait au Sénat: *Cette femme que je produis en témoignage a été l'affranchie et la femme de chambre de ma mère, elle m'a toujours regardé comme son maître. Il y a dans ma maison des gens qui ne s'en usent pas aussi bien.*

"La faiblesse qui ne sait [etc.]."

The italics and variants are Grimm's.

3. Assézat misplaces his reference and thus attributes the aphorism, which is obviously Diderot's own, to both Suetonius and Tacitus.

rot writes in a further addition, "Avancez ou reculez la date d'un événement qui causa l'allégresse publique, et vous produirez la consternation. Voulez-vous entendre les gémissements de la France? Abrégez de quatre à cinq lustres le règne de Louis XIV. Que ne m'est-il permis de montrer, par des exemples moins éloignés, combien les esprits sont diversement affectés selon les moments! Néron meurt exécré; quelques années plus tôt, Néron mourait regretté" (118; I, 169-70). In other words, Nero reigned only a few years too long, whereas Louis XIV outlived his reputation by "quatre à cinq lustres."

In another vein is a long addition concerning occultism, ostensibly in Nero's time. Typically, Diderot begins with the imperfect tense: "Rome alors était pleine d'astrologues et de diseurs de bonne aventure." But as he begins to outline the evil aspects of the phenomenon, he switches to the present: "Le rôle des fourbes qui les professent [les arts mensongers] est de rendre suspects ceux qu'on veut perdre, de divulguer des secrets qu'on veut trahir sans se compromettre; de faire échouer des projects, d'en suggérer; de prévenir, de pressentir le peuple; d'inspirer, de calmer des terreurs: plus le peuple est malheureux, le tyran ombrageux et les grands inquiets, plus on craint l'avenir, plus l'on supporte impatiemment le présent, moins on a d'énergie en soi; plus on a recours aux dieux, plus les arts divinatoires sont en crédit" (138-39; I, 200). The political parallels are obvious; the social ones are perhaps more so.[4] At any rate, again typically, Diderot terminates the passage with a return to Rome and a specific example of the abuse of superstition, but not before causing the reader to think on his own times.

I have just suggested that the political resemblances of

4. Cf. the thesis of Auguste Viatte, *Les sources occultes du romantisme*, Paris, Champion, 1928, 2 vols.

the two ages are complemented by social ones. Parting from Seneca's alleged hypocrisy in associating with the dissipated Serenus, for example, Diderot writes: "Si le vice se couvrit quelquefois dans Rome de l'habit du philosophe, il y fut souvent enveloppé du vêtement sacerdotal. En France, ce ne fut ni dans la magistrature, ni dans l'art militaire, ni dans les académies, ni parmi le peuple, que Molière alla chercher le modèle de l'hypocrite. De son temps, le janséniste reconnaissait le jésuite dans *Tartufe*, et le jésuite y reconnaissait le janséniste; mais, en le montrant sur la scène le cou oblique, les yeux radoucis, le chapeau rabattu, avec le petit collet et le manteau, le poëte ne laissa point de doute sur l'état du personnage" (77; I, 106). He then concludes that in order to evaluate properly the relationship between Seneca and Serenus, it would have been necessary to live in Rome, in fact, in Nero's very court. This relativistic criterion for criticism, while weakening the latter-day critics of Seneca, validates the social commentary of both Molière and Diderot. Perhaps the most effective example of Diderot's growing bitterness, though, is shown in the following citation, which is exactly the same in both editions except for the omission of Paris. "Eh quoi! la justice, la bienfaisance, l'humanité, la patience, la modération, l'héroïsme patriotique ne sont-ils pas dignes de notre admiration et de nos éloges, en quelque lieu que se montrent ou que se soient montrées ces grandes qualités, à Constantinople, à Pékin, à Londres, * dans Athènes l'ancienne, ou dans Rome la moderne?" (164; I, 234-35).[5] The omission seems to be intentional; nor is there any indication that either modesty or rhetorical considerations dictated it.

It must be pointed out that many of the socio-political parallels existed in the 1778 edition. What is to be empha-

5. The asterisk marks the once distinguished position of the French capital. In the 1778 edition the sentence occurs on p. 231.

sized is Diderot's increased disillusionment apparent in the enlarged version of 1782: there are fewer great men in the eighteenth century than in Rome; rulers may not be any more ineffective or tyrannical, but they live longer; superstition and hypocrisy seem worse because they are equally as prevalent in a modern "enlightened" period as in an ancient, notoriously vicious age; and Paris ceases to be a place where national virtues are in evidence.

If there is any doubt as to the depth of Diderot's bitterness, the following observations should eliminate it. In 1778 Diderot at one point merely criticizes Nero's reign, pointing out that tax reform would have assuaged the Roman population, but that Nero chose to suppress their discontent by harsh decrees. The only moral Diderot tries to enunciate is: "Si le prince est bon, ces édits sont inutiles; s'il est méchant, ils sont dangereux: la vraie cuirasse du tyran, c'est l'audace." But in 1782 he openly defends the rights of the people against those of the king: "S'il n'est point de gouvernement où des circonstances urgentes n'exigent l'infraction des lois naturelles, la violation des droits de l'homme et l'oubli des prérogatives des sujets, il n'y en a point où certaines conjonctures n'autorisent la résistence de ceux-ci; d'où naît l'extrême difficulté de définir et de circonscrire avec exactitude le crime de haute trahison. Qui est-ce qui se rendit coupable du crime de lèse-majesté? fut-ce* les Romains ou Néron?" (102-3; I, 144-45).[6] More briefly, less equivocally, Diderot comments on some of Seneca's letters. "Le désespoir des esclaves immole autant d'hommes que les caprices des rois," writes Seneca; and Diderot adds, "Je le désirerais." The Roman asks, "L'esclave a-t-il sur son maître le droit de vie et de mort?" The Frenchman answers, "Qui peut en douter? Puissent tous ces malheureux enlevés, vendus, achetés, revendus, et condamnés au rôle de

6. The asterisk marks a variant (1778): fussent.

la bête de somme, en être un jour aussi fortement persuadés que moi!" (206; II, 11). It is true that in the first edition Diderot hints at revolution, that he even draws a parallel between the welter of superstition immediately preceding Nero's overthrow and the charlatanism of the eighteenth century (168-69; I, 241-42). But only in the second edition does he go so far as to advocate violent overthrow of the existing order, to the extent of placing only one condition against open revolt: "si la révolution ne pouvait guère s'exécuter qu'en faisant couler des flots de sang" (113; I, 162).

It might be assumed from the discussion thus far that on the eve of the Revolution, Diderot is the out-and-out champion of the proletariat. Not at all. Henri Lefebvre has picked up two strong quotations from the first edition, which he believes lead to the opposite conclusion:[7] "L'homme peuple est le plus sot et le plus méchant des hommes: se dépopulariser, ou se rendre meilleur, c'est la même chose." "La voix du philosophe qui contrarie celle du peuple, est la voix de la raison" (263; II, 108; 346). The quotations themselves are misleading; first because Lefebvre combines them into one paragraph, when in all editions of the work they are treated as separate adages; secondly, because he leaves out the third and perhaps the most important of them: "La voix du souverain qui contrarie celle du peuple, est la voix de la folie" (264; II, 109; 347-48); thirdly, because the maxims are paraphrases of Seneca; and lastly, because Diderot himself gently refutes them. Specifically taking issue with Seneca in 1778, he writes: "Les peuples et leurs chefs se doivent un respect mutuel; et, *Faites ce que je vous dis, car tel est mon bon plaisir,*[8] serait la phrase la plus méprisante qu'un monarque pût adresser à ses

7. Henri Lefebvre, *Diderot*, Paris, Hier et Aujourd'hui, 1949, 297.
8. An obvious allusion to Louis XV.

sujets, si ce n'était pas une vieille formule de l'aristocratie transmise d'âge en âge, depuis les temps barbares de la monarchie, jusqu'à ses temps policés" (264; II, 109; 347-48). Thus, in the first edition Diderot is comparatively mild in his approach to the relation of king to people, not only pointing out the need for mutual respect, but also cautiously avoiding direct criticism of Louis XV.

In fact, as Lefebvre points out, Diderot concludes "Il faut laisser subsister la loi" (265; II, 111; 349). If it were possible, usage or custom should be changed, but even this would be undesirable if imposed from above, for acts of despotism, even to a good end, result in an alienation of the rights of the people. Such is obviously not the case in 1782. The two justifications of open revolt cited previously negate the idea of mutual respect; his "Claude n'est rien sur le trône" is an overt and insulting attack on Louis XVI; and the disdain for the people which M. Lefebvre detected is definitely present in the later version.

Describing the interim between the death of Caligula and the ascendance of Claudius, for example, Diderot characterizes the people in these terms: "Délivrés du malheur présent, ils ne savent comment assurer leur bonheur à venir. Le cadavre sanglant du prince assassiné se présente à leur imagination: ils doutent s'ils n'ont pas commis un forfait, ils se troublent, ils s'effrayent; leurs têtes sont étonnées. Sans vues, sans principes, sans plans, s'ils s'occupent de quelque chose, c'est d'échapper aux vengeurs du tyran qui n'est plus, et non de lui donner un digne successeur; d'où il arrive que la mort d'un despote se réduit à conduire au trône un autre despote" (33; I, 36). Impulsive and violent in their acts, the lower classes are indecisive under stress and incapable of providing their own leadership. They are fickle as well: "Voilà le peuple: toujours violent à outrance au moment du crime, toujours compatissant avec sottise au moment de la punition" (90; I, 309 note). And animalistic: "Un des hommes les plus sages que Rome ait produits disait: 'Si les rois sont des bêtes féroces qui dévorent les peuples, quelle bête est-ce donc que le peuple romain qui dévore les rois?' " (64; I, 81). They are vicious as well, for Burrus is still under attack in the eighteenth century, "tant cette énorme bête qu'on appelle le peuple, s'est toujours ressemblé" (111; I, 157). Moreover, they are cowardly; to crush the revolt against him, Nero would only have had to "faire tomber une ou deux têtes" (114; I, 163). To be in their favor is often fatal, as in the case of Octavia, "c'est ainsi que le zèle indiscret du peuple a, dans tous les temps, desservi le mérite et perdu l'innocence" (128; I, 183). In a note to the second edition, Diderot defends the *Apocoloquintosis* as "la satire la plus ingénieuse et la plus vive des honneurs que la bassesse des peuples rendait à leurs tyrans décédés," crowning an already imposing list of unflattering attributes with that of baseness (180; I, 346).

If the lower classes as described in 1782 are impulsive, violent, fickle, animalistic, vicious, inept, cowardly, and base, they have one trait which may be worse, and that is the inability to recognize true worth. Diderot paraphrases and apparently endorses Seneca's description of the sage in retreat: "ils verront sans envie l'admiration du vulgaire prodiguée à des fourbes qui le séduisent, et les récompenses des grands versées sur des bouffons qui les flattent ou qui les amusent" (29; I, 31). At the very best, subservience to public opinion is morally ambigous: "Assurément, le déshonneur est dans l'opinion des hommes, l'innocence est en nous. Ferai-je le mal qu'on approuvera, ou le bien qui sera désapprouvé? Sera-ce la voix du peuple ou celle de ma conscience que j'écouterai? Sages Catons, conseillez-moi" (111; I, 158). The dilemma of the philosopher serving a humanity which does not care or deserve to be so treated is, of course, a typical product of Diderot's paradoxical turn of mind, but it is noteworthy that virtually all of his anti-proletarian comments are found only in the later edition of his work. He does not delete earlier statements to the contrary; in both editions he decries the "monachal spirit" of the stoics and declares, "J'aime le sage en évidence" (221; II, 36; 299). Nor does he modify his harsh judgments of the great. But significantly, he is consistently derogatory of the people when he speaks of them in 1782.

In fact, it certainly seems that he is negative in all the socio-political comments interpolated into the second edition. He spares neither king nor aristocrats, clergy nor people. The increase in bitterness is noticeable on all levels. A power structure that was in 1778 legitimized by the necessity for order is no longer so blessed; a people originally sanctified by its suffering and worthy of being served is hopelessly corrupt. Only the philosopher-public-servant is exempt from criticism, and then, apparently, only if he is Seneca or Diderot, especially Diderot.

A glance at events from 1778 to 1782 will provide political insight enough into the increased pessimism of Diderot's revision of the *Essai*. The young king, whose accendance to the throne had been greeted by a wave of optimism, still had something to his credit in 1778. His dismissal of Maupeou and the firm words of admonition with which he accompanied his restoration of the parlements still stood him in good stead with the *philosophes*. Nor had his administration lost its aura of reform. Though a combination of the parlements, the clergy, the farmers-general, conservative financial interests, and the court had by 1776 brought about the removal from office of the Physiocrat Turgot, he had been replaced by Necker, who was, in reputation at least, no less a liberal reformer than his predecessor. Malesherbes, the tolerant censor who had played such an important role in the publication of the *Encyclopédie*, was given charge of the Maison du Roi in 1775. Sartine, a personal friend of Diderot, was secretary of the navy until 1780, and his reforms went hand in hand with the streamlining and democratization of the military being accomplished by Saint-Germain and his followers. On the foreign scene, finally, the American Revolution was enlisting increased French support as Louis XVI, with Maurepas and especially Vergennes, prudently and skillfully avoided war in Europe.

But by 1782 this picture had altered considerably. The parlements, which for all their claims to enlightenment were essentially a force for conservatism, had discovered that Louis was not ready to back up his resounding words; and the young king found himself as much at odds with the courts as his grandfather had been. The conservative coalition which had brought about Turgot's downfall was a growing power. During the probable time of the revision of the *Essai*, Necker, a genius only in borrowing, was presiding over the continuing decline of national finances, as Malesherbes proved ineffectual and Sartine—and Saint-Germain long before him—joined a parade of disgraced ministers which seemed to progress only in mediocrity.[9] As for the American Revolution, Diderot remains strangely silent about its successes between 1778 and 1782. The note "Aux insurgents de l'Amérique," which had appeared in the original edition, is untouched in the revision, standing in truly Diderotian fashion as a tribute to a nation seeking freedom and a warning not to grow complacent in it.[10]

A final factor to be considered, and one in which Diderot, together with l'abbé Galiani, had shown considerable inter-

9. See Ernest Lavisse, *Histoire de France Illustrée*, Paris, Hachette, 1911, IX, and Alfred Cobban, *A History of Modern France*, Penguin Books, first published 1957, I, 79-148.

10. This note is reproduced, with commentary, in the Garnier edition of Diderot's *Œuvres politiques* (1963).

est, is the wheat question.[11] There had been a poor harvest in 1774, but hope in Louis' new government seemed partially to compensate for the fact, especially in light of Turgot's lifting of restrictions on the wheat trade. The ensuing years had seen no essential improvement in the situation, as bread riots continued to occur around Paris. Indeed, Alfred Cobban and others consider the threat of famine and the ultimate crop failure of 1788 to be a major contributing element to the Revolution.[12] For a person as much involved in current events as was Diderot the evolution of French politics and economics from 1778 to 1782 could hardly have been a source of optimism.

11. *Œuvres politiques*, 61-124.
12. Cobban, 102, 136-38.

5. THE SHIFT
IN THE MORAL CRITERION

In the area of morality, the additions of 1782 do not vary significantly from the original statements of 1778. In both editions moral criteria are relativistic. As Herr Schalk puts it, there is a conscious distinction between public and private morality.[1] Indeed, Pierre Hermand, in his work on Diderot's moral ideas, had already detected this general dichotomy.[2] It is perhaps best expressed in this passage, quoted and requoted since La Harpe first made light of it late in the eighteenth century:

> Il n'y a pas de science plus évidente et plus simple que la morale pour l'ignorant; il n'y en a pas de plus épineuse et de plus obscure pour le savant. C'est peut-être la seule où l'on ait tiré les corollaires les plus vrais, les plus éloignés et les plus hardis, avant que d'avoir posé des principes. Pourquoi cela? C'est qu'il y a des héros longtemps avant qu'il y ait des raisonneurs. C'est le loisir qui fait les uns, c'est la circonstance qui fait les autres: le raisonneur se forme dans les écoles, qui s'ouvrent tard; le héros naît dans les périls, qui sont de tous les temps. La morale est en action dans ceux-ci, comme elle est en maxime dans les poëtes: la maxime est sortie de la tête du poëte, comme Minerve de la tête de Jupiter. . . . Souvent il faudrait un long discours au philosophe pour démontrer ce que l'homme du peuple a subitement senti (313; II, 188; 421-22).[3]

Moral actions are to public heroes what moral maxims are to the poet: spontaneous, complete expressions that are in

1. Schalk, 17.
2. *Les idées morales de Diderot*, Paris, Presses Universitaires de France, 1923.
3. Var. (1778): sent subitement.

conformity with a kind of "volonté générale." But the difficulty of intellectually synthesizing these acts or axioms into a single science is overwhelming. The morality of our acts, says Diderot in a footnote to this passage, is determined by whether or not they are generally approved. But general approval is an unknown, incalculable factor or sum of factors. The mathematical combinations of possible human alternatives and determinants of public reaction are inconceivable, certainly unpredictable.

This materialistic reduction of morality to its simplest terms, as has been stated, does not vary essentially in the two editions; but the nature of the public as interpreted by Diderot has been shown to change considerably. The final judge of morality, the people, is vilified in the second edition. Morality itself, as Diderot defines it, is perhaps not even desirable. Diderot has already been quoted as saying in 1782 that dishonor is public and innocence is in the individual. Politically, the ultimate statement thus is Machiavellian; morally, it is Nietzschean. If this be the "retreat of the sage," it is less stoic than misanthropic or even nihilistic.

To thus sum up the implications of the changes in Diderot's moral stance between the two editions is perhaps to make short shrift of a complex problem; but inasmuch as Diderot's morality has been the topic of many excellent studies, including those of Hermand and Lester Crocker,[4] a separate detailed analysis of that subject has been rejected in favor of a simple indication of the change of Diderot's attitude toward the moral criterion. Room has been, and will be given, moreover, to the moral aspects of the topics considered in this study.

4. Lester Crocker, *Two Diderot Studies, Ethics and Esthetics*, Baltimore, Johns Hopkins Press, 1952.

6. THE CHANGES IN PHILOSOPHICAL ATTITUDE

The term "philosophical" is taken in this chapter of my study in a limited sense to include only the "scientific" and "ethical" aspects of Diderot's world view. "Ethical" is used here to qualify individual or personal criteria of conduct as distinguished from the public or "moral" criterion which has just been established. Mention has already been made of the fundamental optimism of the author's reconsideration of Seneca's *Natural Questions*. In contrast to man's moral side, which presents little or no hope for improvement, his scientific potential is made, in 1782, to appear quite promising. To the old man, study is a source of consolation: "Le vieillard occupé, dont le travail assidu augmentera sans relâche la somme des connaissances, laissera toujours entre le jeune homme et lui à peu près la même différence d'instruction, et la société de celui-ci ne lui déplaira jamais. . . . Lisons donc tant que nos yeux nous le permettront, et tâchons d'être au moins les égaux de nos enfants" (333-34; II, 219). There is optimism even in Diderot's plea for cadavers to be dissected in the medical schools, for the plea itself is a profession of faith in experimental medicine (335-37; II, 221-25).

The ethical side of Diderot's *Essai* is best described by Luppol as a combination of Stoicism and Epicureanism, according to which the individual, in Spinozan fashion, satisfies the needs and desires of his body without violating an intellectual ideal of virtue which is "conforme aux lois de la nature individuelle."[1] According to Luppol, Diderot's "last

1. I. K. Luppol, *Diderot*, Paris, Editions Sociales Internationales, 1936, 323.

33

word" on the subject is this characterization of Stoicism which was, in fact, added in 1782:

"Quand on est inaccessible à la volupté, on l'est à la douleur. . . ." Voilà un de ces corollaires de la doctrine stoïcienne auquel on n'arrive que par une longue chaîne de sophismes. Une statue qui aurait la conscience de son existence serait presque le sage et l'homme heureux de Zénon. . . . "Il faut vivre selon la nature. . . ." Mais la nature, dont la main bienfaisante et prodigue a répandu tant de biens autour de notre berceau, nous en interdit-elle la jouissance? Le stoïcien se refuse-t-il à la délicatesse des mets, à la saveur des fruits, à l'ambroisie des vins, au parfum des fleurs, aux caresses de la femme? . . . "Non; mais il n'en est pas l'esclave. . . ." Ni l'épicurien non plus. Si vous interrogez celui-ci, il vous dira qu'entre toutes les voluptés, la plus douce est celle qui naît de la vertu. Il ne serait pas difficile de concilier ces deux écoles sur la morale. La vertu d'Epicure est celle d'un homme du monde; et celle de Zénon, d'un anachorète. La vertu d'Epicure est un peu trop confiante peut-être; celle de Zénon est certainement trop ombrageuse. Le disciple d'Epicure risque d'être séduit; celui de Zénon, de se décourager. Le premier a sans cesse la lance en arrêt contre la volupté; le second vit sous la même tente, et badine avec elle (315; II, 190-91).

In the final analysis, this is a highly individualistic statement and serves to stress still more Diderot's growing concern with himself. The less positive he is of public approval, the surer he apparently wishes to be of self-esteem. The fact that he prefers the man of the world to the anchorite does not alter his position. Quite the contrary, since the Epicurean, in bantering with sensuality, increases the difficulty and therefore the pleasure of adhering to his private virtue. As Diderot says in an earlier addition, "La raison sans

les passions serait presque un roi sans sujets"(288; II, 151).
His ultimate conclusion would thus be that the individual
must live in society, but by cherishing his own naturally de-
rived ideal of virtue, resist its temptations and disdain its
judgments. All this while serving humanity by the pursuit
of knowledge.

By now it is rather clear that many parts of the *Essai*
are directed to a limited public. Most of the opinions stated
are far from popular, and the advice Diderot gives is often
difficult to interpret. Like Montaigne, to whom he frequently alludes, the eighteenth-century author seems to be
striving for a reconciliation with himself which he is tran-
scribing for the benefit of those few who can appreciate it.

35

7. THE UNITY OF STYLE

The style of the *Essai* presents a complex problem. In the first part Diderot intersperses quotations and paraphrases of Tacitus and Suetonius with his own commentary. His translations are frequently loose, always literary, and his paraphrases often so concise as to be almost unrecognizable as such. There is little or no stylistic distinction between them and Diderot's own commentary. The same is true of the second part, except that the works of Seneca replace those of the historians. To complicate further the question of style there is the editorship of Naigeon, which is and presumably must remain an unknown quantity. Any close stylistic treatment must consequently be restricted to those parts of which Diderot's authorship is quite certain.

From its first appearance the work had the same form, not unlike that of Proust's great novel.[1] At its core is the life of an individual, presented chronologically; but the events or circumstances of that life are often points of departure for the development of a wide range of themes. Each theme is presented, developed, diminished, and later repeated with variations, as in the *Neveu de Rameau*. When Diderot revised the *Essai* he did not, and perhaps even could not, violate its basic form, whence the present-day insistence that the final version is essentially unified. In doubling the length of the work, the author merely extended his development of some of the themes or introduced new variations.

Such has not always been the opinion of critics. Grimm, for one, contrasts the two editions, saying of the second, "Mais si le fonds du livre est beaucoup plus riche qu'il

1. The parallel is immediately suggested by a reading of Poulet's article.

ne l'était, la forme en est aussi plus décousue."² Assézat
agrees: "La première est un travail sévère et qui forme
un ensemble dans lequel il n'y a guère d'autre disparate que
la *note* concernant J.-J. Rousseau. Mais ce fut surtout cette
note qui donna lieu aux reproches qui assaillirent alors
Diderot et le forcèrent à se défendre. La plume une fois re-
prise, il ne sut pas la déposer à temps, et c'est ce qui donne
à cette seconde édition une physionomie indécise et trou-
blée. Le panégyrique de Sénèque et l'apologie de Diderot
s'y confondent trop; et Grimm avait raison de signaler
comme un défaut ce désordre qui porte l'auteur de Paris à
Rome, de Rome à Paris; du règne de Claude à celui de Louis
XV; et de Tacite à l'abbé Royou" (6). The editor concludes that Diderot would have done better to leave the
first edition as it was and publish his response to the critics
separately.³ It might be assumed from such statements that
the additions of 1782 were all direct polemical remarks ad-
dressed to Diderot's contemporaries. As the discussion thus
far has demonstrated, however, this is simply not the case.
True, contemporary allusions are often clearer, and parallels between Paris and Rome more explicit, but there are
numerous interpolations which are only citations from Seneca or the historians, commentaries on these citations, clar-
ifications of historical points, or biographical and cultural
notations. Indeed, except for a few purely polemical passages, such as the attacks on the critics or the justification of
the note on Rousseau, Diderot's additions are almost indis-
tinguishable from his original comments. In other words the
marked difference in tone is not necessarily reinforced by a
change of style. So present-day critics seem to be justified
in declaring the work to be formally unified.

2. *Correspondance littéraire*, XIII, 104.
3. Since Diderot had already published one response to the critics in the
Correspondance littéraire and Marmontel had done his part in refuting them,
it is clear that the author had more in mind than a simple polemic.

DIDEROT'S *Vie de Sénèque*

Herr Schalk's general stylistic characterization of the final version of the *Essai* is valid for the first edition as well.[4] A listing of techniques common to both editions might serve to point up this consistency of style. To evaluate an action Diderot imagines a dialogue between two interested persons (30-31; I, 33; 34) (107-8; I, 150-52).[5] As an indication that tyranny does not change its nature, he attributes the words or traits of a Bourbon to a Caesar (36-38; I, 40-42; 44-46).[6] So that the relation of past to present will be more striking he frequently switches from one tense to another. By an uncharacteristically frequent use of images he confuses his own style with that of Seneca.[7] In juxtaposing ancient and contemporary personalities he inevitably elicits a comparison.[8] The repetition at the beginning of different topics of the phrase "n'est plus" with different subjects suggests that history is cyclical and that human attributes are unchanging.[9] The Nero-tiger association is consistently used to show the danger inherent in serving the emperor. In fact, all the stylistic devices for which Diderot has been alternately blamed and praised are present in both editions. This fact, and the fact also that there are numerous stylistic variants which could be shown only in a critical edition, indicate strongly that Diderot intended the second version to be a single unified work, with its "défense" an integral part of it.

If this is indeed the case, then the logical conclusion would be that the work in its final form is a broader, more

4. Schalk, 22-23. It is doubtful that Herr Schalk would entirely agree with my opinion.
5. The first parentheses refer to a quotation which was in the original edition, the second, in the revision alone.
6. Both Claudius and Louis XVI were treated as imbeciles when they were children.
7. He frequently quotes, and pauses to admire, Seneca's metaphors.
8. If the comparisons are more explicit in 1782, they are no more frequent.
9. "Rousseau n'est plus," "Le monstre n'est plus," "Sénèque n'est plus," etc.

38

inclusive statement than the original; for the first edition is not refuted, it is enlarged, and its tenets, rather than being negated, are qualified. Before a final pronouncement can be made, though, one last aspect of the *Essai*, its personal side, must be examined.

8. THE CHANGES
IN PERSONAL ATTITUDE

Just as there is an obvious attempt on Diderot's part to draw parallels between Paris and Rome, so there is a noticeable *rapprochement* between the lives of Seneca and Diderot. Mr. Loy states their basic points of comparison and M. Fabre suggests others.[1] Besides these similarities there are others of a personal nature which may be more than co-incidental. Both Seneca and Diderot had fathers worthy of respect, both had brothers who were apparently preferred by the father. Both were "hommes nouveaux," or first-generation philosophers from a generally undistinguished but solid lineage. Both sought and were refused parental approval for their chosen profession, and both experienced political persecution as a result of their choice. If the close resemblance is accepted, it would then seem legitimate to ask, as does M. Fabre, whether in justifying Seneca, Diderot is justifying himself. Essentially Seneca is charged with greed, hypocrisy, cowardice, dishonor, and bad writing. If Diderot was ever open to these accusations, the probability that he was writing his own apology is further increased.

There is in both editions of the *Essai* a marked preoccupation with wealth and the moral aspects of obtaining it and disposing of it. Diderot's approach does not significantly change and may be summed up as follows: wealth as such is neither good nor evil, but the attitude toward it may be; what is important is that prosperity be a matter of complete indifference to the sage; and the test of this indifference is the manner in which money is used. Specifically, "La

1. Loy, 248. See the discussion, 396-99, for M. Fabre's observations.

richesse de Sénèque,[2] prodigeuse pour un simple parti-
culier . . . exorbitante pour un philosophe," was not the
result of Seneca's greed, but of fate: "il n'alla[3] point à elle,
il la reçut quand elle vint à lui" (148; I, 211; 207). In short,
Seneca inherited from his father a fortune which was increased by the astute management of Helvia, his mother,
to immense proportions. It was further increased by unsolicited gifts from Nero, but never became a preoccupation with the philosopher. Used primarily and often
anonymously for the benefit of his friends and family, it
nevertheless was a source of envy for malicious minds, especially Suilius and Dion Cassius (148-58; I, 211-25; 207-18).
In the two editions there are repeated references to
Seneca's fortune, all of them describing his disinterest or
generosity, or attacking his detractors. The points of coin-
cidence are clear: although Diderot's personal fortune, ac-
quired late in his life, could not compare in size with that of
Seneca, it was comfortable. A large part of it was inherited
from his father and was competently managed by Diderot
and his sister until it became sizeable. Unsolicited gifts from
Catherine and others augmented it still more. Needless to
say, it was used generously, especially in the marriage of
his daughter. Whether or not he was personally attacked
for the financial transactions of his later years (and he was,
particularly for the sale of his library), there is every indication that he was somewhat uneasy about them.[4] And the
fact that the attack on Suilius, "un délateur vénal et formidable, un scélérat justement exécré de la multitude des
citoyens, un prévaricateur, un concussionnaire," immedi-

2. Var. (1778): Cette richesse.
3. Var. (1778): alloit.
4. Besides the financial by-play with Catherine, there were the negotiations
for a marriage contract. See Arthur Wilson, *Diderot: The Testing Years,
1713-1759*, New York, Oxford, 1957, 345. Also Crocker, *Embattled Philosopher*, 361-66, 390.

ately precedes the note on Rousseau, who is variously described as "un artificieux scélérat . . . l'homme atroce . . . le lâche," at the very least introduces the possibility that Diderot might have feared further criticism of his financial interests.

To return to the comparison of the two editions, I have said that Diderot's basic position does not change significantly in the four years separating them. There is, however, one new note added, that of practicality. Praising Diogenes, Seneca comments, "celui qui doute de son bonheur, peut aussi douter de la félicité des dieux, qui n'ont ni argent ni propriété," and Diderot interjects, somewhat cynically: "ni besoin" (311; II, 184-85). It is true that in 1778 he says that to scorn the necessary is madness, but he describes the necessary as bread and water: "Je voudrais bien savoir où est la honte de ne pas vouloir mourir de soif et de faim" (273; II, 125; 365). But in 1782 he is able to say: "Il ne faut pas calomnier la prospérité; le bonheur n'est pas toujours un signe du mépris des dieux" (298; II, 164). The word "besoin" has thus changed somewhat to include both money and property and to be qualified even as prosperity. It thus seems fair to say that whether Diderot would admit it or not, the monetary affairs of his later life left their mark. His constant apology, not only for relative comfort, but for actual prosperity, seems personal, and, more than coincidentally, makes a sharp contrast with the continued ill fortune and proclaimed asceticism of Jean-Jacques Rousseau.

Friendship is another personal theme of the *Essai*. In the preface to the first edition Diderot makes the statement, "Assez voisin du terme où tout s'évanouit, je n'ambitionnais que l'approbation de ma conscience et le suffrage de quelques amis" (9; I, 2; 6). So, consistently, he speaks warmly of friends and friendship throughout the early version. Discussing Seneca's opinion that the man who cares only to satisfy his needs "ne se morfond point à la porte des grands," Diderot advises, "Frappez à cette porte pour autrui, n'y frappez jamais pour vous" (202; II, 5; 276). A certain plaintive note is struck when he gently reminds the reader of his own notorious generosity: "combien d'hommes ont plutôt manqué d'amis que d'amitié," but on the following page he recants, eloquently. "[Sénèque] prétend qu'on refait aussi aisément un ami perdu, que Phidias une statue brisée. Je n'en crois rien. Quoi! l'homme à qui je confierai mes pensées les plus secrètes, qui me soutiendra dans les pas glissants de la vie, qui me fortifiera par la sagesse de ses conseils et la continuité de son exemple; qui sera le dépositaire de ma fortune, de ma liberté, de ma vie, de mon honneur . . . cet homme se refait en un jour, en un mois, en un an! Eh! malheureusement la durée de la vie y suffit à peine; et c'est un fait bien connu des vieillards, qui aiment mieux rester seuls, que de s'occuper à retrouver un ami" (207; II, 13; 279-80). Near the end of the 1778 edition he proclaims his intellectual friendship for Seneca, and adds, "Si j'ai le malheur de vivre assez longtemps pour perdre ceux qui me sont chers, Sénèque, Plutarque, Montaigne et quelques autres, viendront souvent adoucir l'ennui de la solitude où mes amis m'auront laissé . . ." (367; II, 269; 488).

At the age of sixty-five, then, he still hopes to win the approval of a few friends, he can still wax eloquent over the idea of friendship, he still has friends, and counts on losing them only through death. The note on Rousseau alone gives any hint of bitterness, but the treachery of the unnamed "scélérat" is rather abstract and universal than personal.

Four years later, he is still capable of being moved by the spectacle of friendship: "J'ai vu l'amour, j'ai vu l'amitié héroïque; le spectacle des deux amis m'a plus touché que celui des deux amants. D'un côté c'était la raison, de l'autre

43

la passion, qui faisait de grandes choses: l'homme et l'animal" (205; II, 9). But treachery masquerading as friendship touches him more: "Quelle étrange révolution les années ont apportée dans mon caractère! Lorsque j'entends Agamemnon dire à Iphigénie:

> Vous y serez, ma fille,

je suis encore touché; mais lorsque j'entends Auguste dire à un perfide:

> Soyons amis, Cinna,

mes yeux se remplissent de larmes" (291; II, 154). He repeats, "On ne refait donc pas un ami, comme Phidias une statue brisée" (303; II, 172).[5] But the statement by its very repetition has taken on a new force. It is final and self-contained. Instead of being placed in the context of a passionate evocation of what friendship is, it follows an axiomatic statement by Seneca that friends are rare and difficult to find. Friendship has become "la passion de la jeunesse." The selflessness, the instinctive communication of feelings and ideas, the sharing of mind and matter are things of the past: "Qu'est devenue cette maniére d'exister si une, si violente et si douce? A peine m'en souviens-je; l'intérêt personnel l'a successivement affaiblie. Je suis vieux, et je m'avoue, non sans amertume et sans regret, qu'on a des liaisons d'habitude dans l'âge avancé; mais qu'il ne reste en nous, à côté de nous, que le vain simulacre de l'amitié" (204; II, 9). At sixty-nine he has become the old man who prefers to remain alone. There is one friend left, oneself: "c'est toi; tâche d'être ton meilleur ami."

One rather striking variant seems to sum up the change which occurred during the four years separating the two

5. Var.: Assézat, following Naigeon and Brière, punctuates with a question mark.

editions. In 1778 he concludes his portrait of the persecuted philosopher-politician with the words, "Préférez le repos, vivez avec vos amis et avec vos livres: dans les temps de peste on se renferme." In 1782 he changes "vos amis" to "vous-même." True, Diderot is ostensibly paraphrasing the advice of Seneca to the prospective public-servant, but the portrait is too much like Diderot's opinion of himself to be mistaken, especially the part added in 1782: "vos subalternes vous trahiront, vos prôneurs vous feront des ennemis, vos enthousiastes vous nuiront; vous serez malhonnêtement attaqué, peut-être trop vivement défendu . . ." (243; II, 74; 313-14). Add to this the personal pique which characterizes the diatribe against Rousseau and you have a man completely disillusioned with personal relationships.

What actually transpired between him and his friends in the four years is minimal. Rousseau had been dead a little longer, Grimm had drifted away physically as well as spiritually, d'Alembert had long been out of touch, Sophie Volland had become less important to him. He had, in fact, very little close contact with anyone except his family. The change in perspective, then, seems almost to be the result of brooding on his past, thinking about the permanent value of his intimate experiences. The fact that he deletes almost none of the earlier, warmer passages only serves to enhance the truly human dilemma of having lived and loved as fully as possible and still being incapable of philosophizing from such experience. All of his impressions are true, none of them is predominant: a friend is a friend is a friend. But the biographical fact remains: while Diderot was mostly warm and gentle in 1778 when he wrote about friendship, in 1782 he was bitter and disappointed.

9. THE SPECTER
OF POSTERITY

Perhaps the most personal of all Diderot's concerns in the *Essai* is his reputation. Whether he is proclaiming his disinterest, denying the validity of public opinion, raking over the critics, or surrendering himself and his writings to the will of the future public, he never stops worrying about his "image." Both editions contain numerous passages on personal repute, and here again a difference in attitude is detectable. In 1778 he seems almost serene in regard to posterity, agreeing with Seneca's opinion that "le sage qui craint l'opinion, ressemble à un général qui s'ébranle à la vue d'un nuage de poussière élevé par un troupeau" (208; II, 15; 282). When the Roman pronounces that one must never excite hatred, envy, or scorn, his commentator retorts, "il y a des hommes dont il est glorieux d'être haï; le tourment de l'envie est toujours un éloge; le mépris n'est souvent qu'une affectation." And to the warning, "Craignons l'admiration," Diderot responds, "Et pourquoi? Faisons tout ce qui peut en mériter" (209; II, 17; 284). He applauds Epicurus' disdain of public opinion (219; II, 32; 296). He claims to desire the praises only of those whose reproaches he fears (241; II, 71; 311). Denouncing Seneca's "monastic" and "anti-social" views he embraces an attitude of indifference to the "foule": "C'est une sotte vanité que de s'affliger ou de s'offenser quand elle [la foule] ne vient pas; c'est ajouter à l'éclat que de la repousser quand elle vient. Et qu'importe qu'on parle ou qu'on se taise de vous, pourvu que vous vous retiriez à temps? Le malade craint-il ou souhaite-t-il qu'on dise qu'il s'est mis au lit?" (242; II, 73; 313). In a number of passages he claims to be impervious to all opinion, even that of posterity. Aware that he will be maligned, he is still confident that justice will triumph: "Un jour viendra où les libelles publiés contre les hommes les plus illustres de ce siècle seront tirés de la poussière par des méchants animés du même esprit qui les a dictés; mais il s'élèvera, n'en doutons point, quelque homme de bien indigné qui décèlera la turpitude de leurs calomniateurs, et par qui ces auteurs célèbres seront mieux défendus et mieux vengés que Sénèque ne l'est par moi" (270; II, 120; 359). Moreover, it is the fate of the *philosophe* to suffer: "Vous serez persécuté; c'est votre destinée; on vous fera boire la ciguë, Socrate l'a bien bue avant vous; on vous emprisonnera, on vous exilera, on brûlera vos ouvrages, on vous fera peut-être vous-même monter sur un bûcher." But again, in Diderot's case, those who can hurt him, won't, and those who wish to, can't (271; II, 122-23; 261). In any event, he still finds it difficult to decide whether to serve humanity or his country, "être l'homme de tous les temps, ou l'homme de son siècle? C'est un problème difficile à résoudre" (325; II, 206; 441-42).

The conclusion of the first edition bears out the serenity of his attitude toward fame. Personally he hopes only to inspire the horror of calumny and veneration for the great man wronged: "moins jaloux que l'homme de génie retrouvât en lui quelques-unes de mes pensées, que flatté, si l'homme de bien se reconnoissoit dans mes sentiments."[1] Generally, he sums up the work with an observation by a British scholar, who, after visiting the monuments to Seneca, compared them to Nero's palace: "La curiosité du voyageur est la même, mais les sentiments qu'il éprouve

---

1. This sentence, which occurs at the end of the first edition (p. 518), appears in the preface of the second edition, but somewhat rearranged: "beaucoup moins flatté que l'homme de génie se retrouvât dans quelques-unes de mes pensées, que s'il arrivait à l'homme de bien de se reconnaître dans mes sentiments."

47

sont bien différents; ici, il voit l'image de la vertu; là il erre au milieu des spectres du crime: il plaint et bénit le Philosophe; il maudit le Tyran" (192; I, 275-76; 517-19).[2] All in all he seems displeased with neither his lot nor its rewards.

There is an immeasurable difference between this conclusion and that of 1782. In 1778 Diderot seems to be supremely confident that whatever the opinion of the multitudes, which may even approve of him, he will be well remembered by those of his contemporaries who are important to him and by a posterity which will recognize his contributions to his nation and to humanity. In 1782 he removes his last two paragraphs to a less prominent place in the text and appends in their place forty pages of polemic, which prove, if nothing else, that contemporary opinion is more important to him than he has thought and that his future reputation may, after all, be permanently damaged by the critics. Nor does his justification of the note on Rousseau betray the serenity with which he earlier contemplated his own posterity. There seems little doubt that Diderot's confidence in the future was severely jolted by the personal and public circumstances of the four years separating the two editions.

A curious sidelight to this self-consciousness is the distinction Diderot consistently makes between a "belle action" and a "belle page." In both editions he prefers the former to the latter, but he affirms the preference twice as often in 1782 as in 1778. He seems to have been increasingly convinced that his eventual reputation would not be based on his literary achievements, possibly not even on his philosophical contributions, but rather on his personal courage and humanitarian views. So Lucan the parricide destroys Lucan the poet, the eloquence of Jean-Jacques is over-

2. I have exceptionally quoted from the first edition to show the capitalization of the last two substantives. Cf. Assézat for variants.

shadowed by his treachery, the rehabilitator of Calas is more admired than the author of *Mahomet*. By extension we are presumably asked to judge Diderot the man, not the writer, and to evaluate him as he did Seneca, in the context of his times.

So, in his personal reflections, Diderot comments on the alleged greed, hypocrisy, and poor style of Seneca. There appears little doubt from the preceding discussion that the apologist was, or felt himself to be, open to the same charges, and that his reaction to them was stronger in 1782 than in 1778. On the other two counts, cowardice and dishonor, there can be only speculation. Suffice it to say that Seneca's return from exile and Diderot's release from Vincennes were effected under somewhat questionable circumstances.[3] Is it not possible that the sometimes violent and ill-disguised attacks on the Bourbons were latter-day attempts to avoid the very charges just mentioned? Did not Diderot, after all, feel called upon to renounce his own forty-year-old castigation of Seneca? One thing is clear: Diderot in both versions of the *Essai* is sensitive to criticism, and more so in the second than in the first. The spectacle of Seneca, calumniated by his contemporaries and by an equally vicious posterity, might well have made his apologist reflect on the dubious circumstances of his own life and wonder of what crimes he himself might be accused.

3. Wilson, 105-9.

10. PHILOSOPHY
AND THE MAN

The Diderot of the *Essai* is generally pictured, no doubt largely because of his own self-portrait in the preface to the first part, as calmly facing death, grateful for the moments of serene meditation that remain to him, learning from Seneca the secrets of inner peace, in short, satisfied with his own career. A comparison of the two editions negates the image. Certainly in the changes that have been discussed, the general impression is the opposite. Not only is he distressed with the political and social evils of his times, he is also tortured by personal doubts and fearful of his reputation, present and future. What a picture he gives: the king is weak, the government corrupt, the people fickle and superstitious, Paris devoid of greatness; critics are hateful and misinformed, friends are treacherous, and, most important of all, even posterity, in whom, when he wrote his famous *Lettres à Falconet*, he had once so much confidence, is not to be trusted. Diderot is an island of honesty in a sea of perfidy. Marmontel rises to his defense, but Marmontel's comments need to be amplified, and he is outnumbered.

The comparison begs to be made. There is something profoundly human, profoundly significant in the almost simultaneous appearance of Rousseau's confession and Diderot's apology, both of which are posited on the frailty of the individual man. Two of the greatest men of their century betray an overriding concern with what other men think of them. Both, in so doing, reveal a sense of insecurity which belies their professed self-assurance. Both at heart blame for their ills a social structure which, thanks largely to them, will be destroyed in the name of humanity. If the *Essai* is less great than the *Confessions*, less significant in the history of letters, less eloquent, and deservedly less famous, it is none the less revelatory of a great man and his times. What is most striking about both works is, of course, the personality involved. There is, however, this great difference: whereas Rousseau's work is inevitably psychological in motivation, Diderot's is basically intellectual.

Diderot reconstructing the life of Seneca is not unlike Sartre's Roquentin in *La Nausée*, writing the biography of Rollebon. The more he tries to derive significance and order from an individual's existence, the less he succeeds. Finally, overwhelmed by the inconsistencies of Seneca's life, writings, and reputation, Diderot changes his tack. Whereas in 1778 he wrote as if he could really justify Seneca, or himself, basing the *Essai sur la vie de Sénèque* on the assumption that wrong will eventually be righted, in the *Essai sur les règnes de Claude et de Néron* he assumes nothing; he merely poses a problem. As in *Jacques le fataliste*, he supplies no conclusion. The difference between the two editions may thus be summed up as follows. In 1778 Diderot sat down to write his swan song, a Stoic-Epicurean hymn to virtue and its eventual rewards. He seemed ready to die the "death of Socrates" which had always fired his imagination.[1] Both the critical reaction to his work, however, and, no doubt, the nature of the attacks made against Seneca by an ungracious posterity, prompted a revision. The result is an anthem to the misunderstood genius, a combination of social criticism and glorification of the individual which was to become only too familiar fifty years later. The *Essai sur les règnes de Claude et de Néron* is testimony to the truth of Diderot's defense of one of Seneca's human failings: "La philosophie n'anéantit pas l'homme."

1. See Jean Seznec, *Essais sur Diderot et l'antiquité*, Oxford, Clarendon Press, 1957, 1-22.

51

UNIVERSITY OF FLORIDA MONOGRAPHS

Humanities